THE WASTEPAPER BASKET ARCHIVE

THE WASTEPAPER BASKET ARCHIVE

By

Simon Brett

Illustrations

Wendy Hutton

SIDGWICK & JACKSON

LONDON

First published in 1986
by Sidgwick and Jackson Limited
Copyright © 1986 Simon Brett
Designed by Wendy Hutton

ISBN 0-283-99242-5

Printed and bound in Great Britain by
Biddles Ltd, Guildford and King's Lynn
for Sidgwick & Jackson Limited
1 Tavistock Chambers, Bloomsbury Way, London WC1A 2SG

CONTENTS

INTRODUCTION

The value of documentation in the study of history and of contemporary life has long been recognised, and the historian and social commentator frequently find the unofficial documents of the famous more revealing than their authorised statements. How much more telling, in the consideration of eminent characters, is what they have rejected than what they have willingly released to the world.

It is from these unofficial sources that THE WASTEPAPER BASKET ARCHIVE has been compiled. Exhaustive research, and modern retrieval methods have made it possible to present to the public this unique collection of private papers. Whether the item recovered be a letter, a discontinued early draft or a mere fragment, each one of them offers a new - and frequently unexpected - insight into the personality of the relevant wastepaper basket's owner.

"To Peter Titheradge."

VR

17th February
1840

Albert—

We were amused
by what you did last
night.
Present yourself at the
Royal Bedchamber
this evening at 9:45
precisely and we (you)
will try it another way.

Victoria Regina

(And no more of
your naughty
spoonerisms Albert
Those are'nt amusing
they're just vulgar!)

THE WRITEWAY SCHOOL OF NOVEL-WRITING

(CORRESPONDENCE COURSES TO HELP YOU IMPROVE YOUR STYLE AND LEARN HOW TO WRITE STUFF THAT´LL REALLY SELL!)

LESSON ONE :

The most important thing for any writer to learn is how to tell a JOLLY GOOD STORY.

But the best writers also manage to TELL A JOLLY GOOD STORY IN AN INTERESTING WAY.

And what are the magic ingredients that helps you TELL A JOLLY GOOD STORY IN AN INTERESTING WAY? Well, first of all, there´s a little secret called STYLE. And then there´s another thing called HAVING BELIEVABLE, THREE-DIMENSIONAL CHARACTERS.

So the first aim of this course is to teach you how to develop your own STYLE - to avoid flatness, dullness... well, we don´t need to detail all the things that are often wrong with people´s STYLE. The fact that you´ve enrolled in this correspondence course means that you´re well aware of your own shortcomings in that direction!

Right, so what are your first steps going to be in stopping your writing being turgid and boring? Before anything else, just try READING SOMETHING YOU´VE WRITTEN. Yes, it may be a bit of a shock - not to say rude awakening. Why is it that yo~~~~~~~~~ alive, can´t make them jump~~~~~ interesting way?

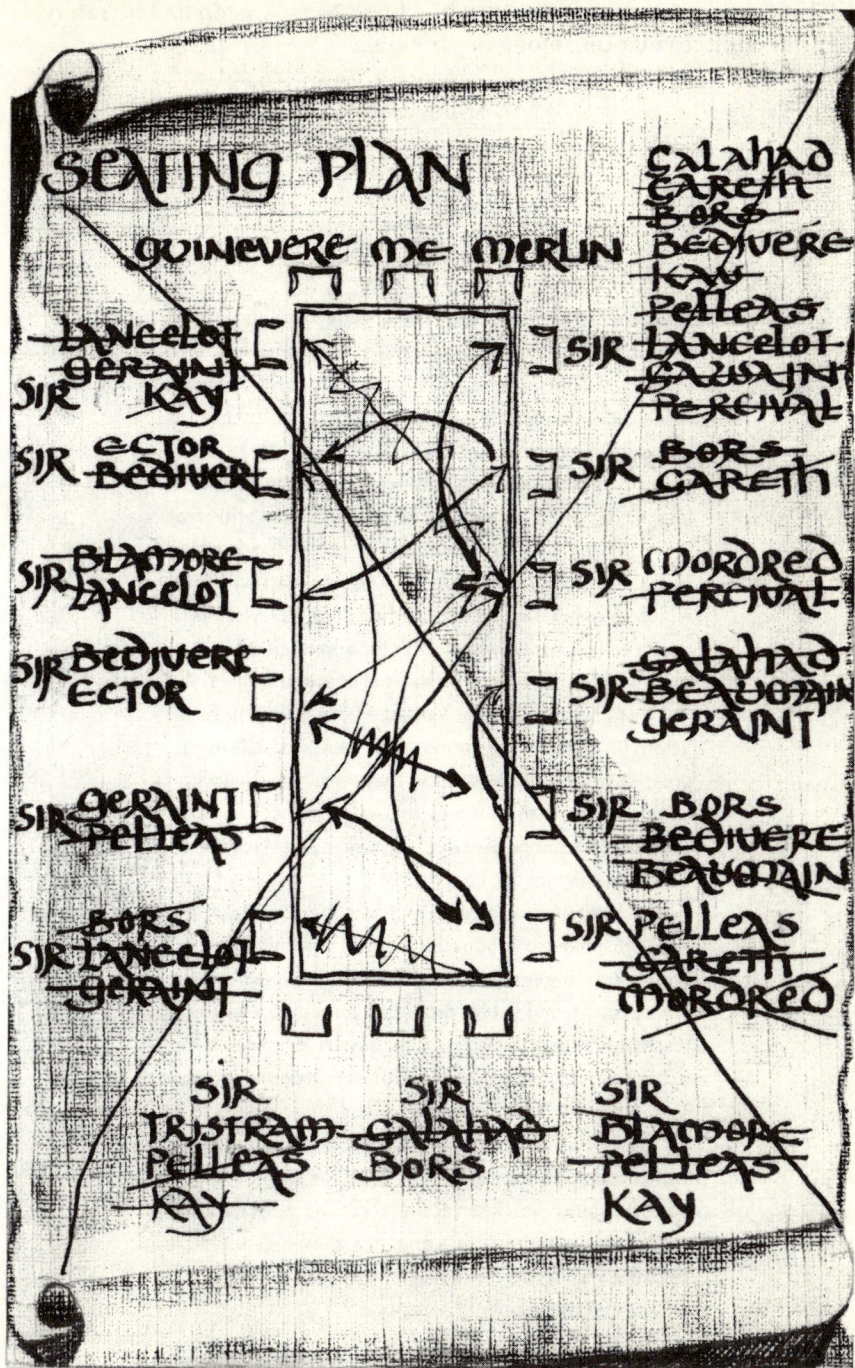

From JANE AUSTEN'S WASTEPAPER BASKET

This fragment appears to be part of a book Miss Austen had privately printed for circulation among her friends.

SENSE AND SENSUALITY

CHAPTER ONE

It is a truth universally acknowledged, that a single woman in possession of her virginity, must be in a state of urgency to lose it. Such was the condition of Arabella Moreton, in whom the becoming modesty of infancy:- a reticence of participation in boys' plays - gave way, at fifteen, to much talk of the proximity of the Regiment, and a longing for balls; though these passions were still tempered by a maidenly bashfulness, which disguised an inclination for more heroic enjoyments; an inclination which grew as she entered her twentieth year to a constant excitation; and which, with the approach of her thirtieth birthday, fell but little short of desperation.

The family of Moreton had long been settled in Kent. Though Arabella's parents were not invited to the greatest houses of the county, they were nonetheless on calling terms with many of the lesser gentry; amongst whom the exchange of cards, courtesies, and occasionally wives, was the invariable practice.

Mr. Moreton was a gentleman of considerable aspirations; in mixed company he was all eager delight;- his hands were here, there, everywhere, when young ladies were present; and yet his profligacy remained a matter of discussion rather than execution. As Mrs. Moreton knew, to her cost, despite her own continued exertion of strength and ingenuity, her husband had long since ceased to be an equal participant in those intimacies of marriage, which religion has endowed with its blessing. Like the boastful soldier of classical literature, he devoted a disproportionate number of words to something, which, in his case, was of such minor significance, that it did not in truth merit the dignity of a mention.

1

SENSE AND SENSUALITY

For many wives, this situation might be regarded as a matter for regret, but as one incapable of improvement: an opportunity, perhaps, for a more rigorous concentration on the arts of the needle, the pencil, and the piano; or for the more intense pursuit of those interferences in the lives of the underprivileged, which pass under the title of charity. Mrs. Moreton was not such a woman. When it became clear to her that her expectations within the confines of marriage were reduced to mere civilities, she turned her eye outward, in the hope - nay, indeed, with the firm intention, - of meeting a gentleman of more dependable endowments, whose inclination towards misconduct would match her own.

In this quest, she was quickly satisfied; making the acquaintance of a Mr. Bolney, a gentleman of unimpeachable parts; husband of a lady, who, from lack of interest rather than lack of ability, manifested the same marital shortcoming as Mr. Moreton. Communication was quickly established; and mutual compliment soon transformed this into intimacy; for, when waning charms and flattery are united, it requires uncommon steadiness of reason to resist the attraction of being called the most charming creature in the world. Under such circumstances, a lapse from grace must be reckoned inevitable; particularly when, as in this case, lapsing from grace is, on both sides, already a firm intention.

A regular sequence of *rendezvous* became as nearly settled, as the nature of such arrangements would allow. In the name of card games, and of the healthful necessity of taking as much fresh air as the constitution will accept, Mrs. Moreton and Mr. Bolney contrived to meet with the regularity of church services. Their respective spouses, for reasons of either stupidity or tactics, remained unaware of this exceedingly convenient arrangement; though both benefited from the increased geniality and greater ease, which their partners' behaviour manifested.

2

Though, to Mr. Moreton, his wife's new interest remained unknown, it did not escape the observation of Arabella's increasingly spinsterish eye. The discovery brought to her a melange of new feelings; dejection, mortification, anxiety, resentment, and offence, quickly ceding their place to a restlessness of spirit, which she knew could be defined as nothing more nor less than jealousy. If her mother could so easily, and without punishment, succumb to such indulgences, why should they be denied to Arabella herself.

Nor did she lack for other models of behaviour within the confines of her own family. Arabella was the eldest of two sisters; and Cecily, her junior, had shown no diffidence in organising that most important aspect of a young girl's life, which caused her sister such unnecessary perturbation. At seventeen Cecily had eloped to Bath with a handsome young lieutenant from the Regiment quartered nearby, and, when he had abandoned her after two months, she had elected to stay within those fine and striking environs. There, by frequent attendance at the Pump-room, she developed a facility of mixing in the society of gentlemen of all ages; many of whom, charmed by the ease of her address, would, after an appropriate interval, call at her lodgings in Milsom-street; where the smiling and affectionate manner of her greeting, encouraged many to stay, and, with great felicity, to offer money for the privilege. Cecily accepted these kindnesses with gratitude, and was a living demonstration to her elder sister, that, though its propriety might not be commensurate with its pleasantness, such a manner of existence could be a source, not only of enjoyment, but also of considerable profit.

Arabella, then, did not lack models for behaviour; but as yet she lacked that object so essential to all young ladies burdened as she was: a gentleman willing to introduce her to the manners and customs of that country,

3

which she so earnestly desired to visit, but which at times seemed forever to be locked to her.

Arabella was neither weak, nor irresolute, nor lacking in mental endowments. She compared her life with that of her sister; and quickly observed the truth: that, while her own misfortune was a lack of one gentleman, Cecily's only conceivable affliction was an excess of masculine addresses. Arabella resolved, therefore, to arrange a more even distribution of her sister's riches; and, vowing that, in the two months which remained before her thirtieth birthday, she would lose that thing whose continued presence had become such a source of irritation to her, set out for Bath.

4

Banquo and Fleance

Macbeth and Lady Macbeth

at Hame

12th December 1040 · 7.0 for 7.30

R.S.V.P.
·· The Palace
Forres ··

Come as you are!

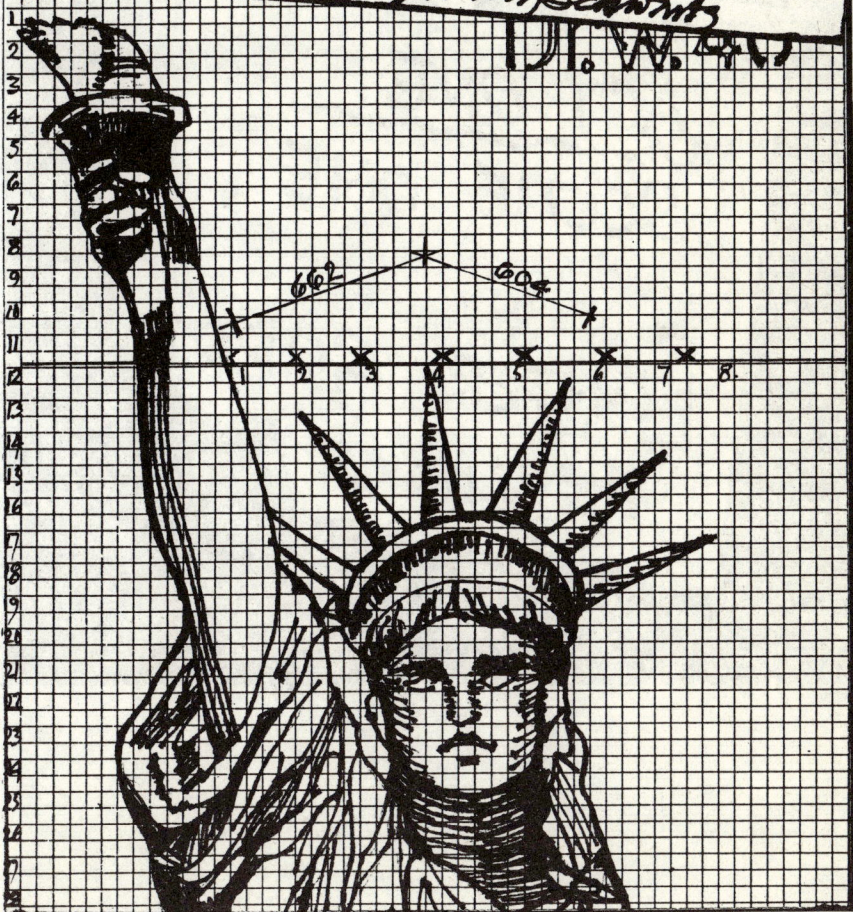

Dear Mr Bartholdi

Many thanks for submitting your design. I am afraid, to be quite honest, here at the agency we had envisaged something a little less flamboyant for the launch of "Frizzi Ice Cream Bumper Cornet". I apologise to you for all the time and hard work you must have spent on the design, and hope that you may be able to place it somewhere else.

Yours

Irving Schwartz

It was a lovely day as Little Noddy parked his jolly little yellow car outside Big Ears' house. The little bell on his hat jingled cheerily as he walked up the garden path and rat-a-tat-tatted on Big Ears' door. "How nice to see you, Noddy," said Big Ears as he opened the door. "Do come in and sit down."

Noddy went in and sat down on Big Ears' jolly, plump, comfy sofa. Big Ears sat down beside him.

"What shall we do on such a lovely day?" asked Noddy.

"Well, I've got a few ideas," said Big Ears. And do you know - naughty old Big Ears put his hand on Little Noddy's knee.

"You know," said Noddy, "there's one thing I've always wondered about you, Big Ears."

"Oh yes?" said Big Ears.

"It's about your name. I mean,it's a jolly unusual name, isn't it? You haven't even got particularly big ears."

"Well, no, it's a euphemism, isn't it?" said Big Ears.

"A what?" asked Little Noddy.

"Well, a euphemism is like when you say something polite, meaning something that's jolly well not polite," said Big Ears. "I mean, people say my ears are big, but they don't mean my ears at all."

"Oh. What do they mean?" asked Little Noddy.

"I'll show you," said Big Ears and he unbuttoned

On the 8th of October we drank tea with
Mrs Thrale, Sir Joshua Reynolds and
Dr Goldsmith were also of the company,
and we discussed the precedence of
Life over Literature ~

Goldsmith "Which would you prefer sir?"

Johnson "Don't know"

Goldsmith "Nay sir, but if you were
forced to an opinion"

Johnson "Never thought about it"

The conversation then took another turn

Reynolds "Sir, do you agree with what
Voltaire has written on the subject?"

Johnson "Haven't read it. Who did
you say?"

Reynolds "Voltaire"

Johnson "Never heard of him"

Boswell "But do you not think Sir,
that Literature is the finest
flowering of human genius?"

Johnson "No"

Boswell "What, then, Sir, may take
that title?"

Johnson "No idea"

Mrs Thrale then asked for his opinion
on religion, but Johnson said
he had none. On politicks he had
nothing to say, and when

Possible Titles

Heathcliff and Cathy

Cathy and Heathcliff

The Earnshaw Saga

It's a Reet Grand Life

Wuthering Heights

Moor or Less

Cathy and Edgar

The Country Diary of an Emotional Lady

The Earnshaw Concession

The Secret Diary of Hareton Heathcliff aged 13 3/4

I like this one Emily Branwell.

Mayhem on the Moors

The Hitchhikers Guide to Yorkshire

Oh No! It's The Heacliffs!

How Green was my Moor

It Ain't Half Windy, Mum

Carry On Wuthering

Cathy Come Home

Together Forever

Forever Together

IDEA FOR A NOVEL ?
(Alma ?)

Girl / living in London
flat has lots of friends
(Christopher ?)
Meets man / at work
— She falls in love with
him
He falls in love with her.
Their parents and friends
get on well together.
They get married and
live very happily together, -
still with lots of friends ?
A bit unplausible.

As I walked through the wilderness of this world, I lighted on a certain place where was a Den and I laid me down in that place to sleep: and as I slept I dreamed a dream, I dreamed and behold I saw a girl clothed but in a shift, standing with her legges apart, with a face that looked like she knew what it was all about, a couple of buttons undone at the top, and a great paire of tittes, I looked and saw her open her lippes and licke them, and as she did, she sighed and trembled; and not being able longer to contain myself, I brake out with a mighty cry saying Cor! Gette 'em off I could fancy a bit right, now! And needed a couple more and reached her throb

To The Cleaning Lady.

Dear Mrs P. – I am sorry 'bout the mess.
But you know how it is when once I start.
Please tidy up, and make it more or less
Presentable, if not exactly smart.
I'm sorry for the stains of bouillabaisse
And where I spilled the plum and
                            raspberry tart;
And also for that mash of peas and carrot
And where I overturned my glass of claret.

Ignore the drunken snorer in the chair –
He is a friend – God damn it!
                    What's his name? –
And just pick up the Lady's underwear –
(I can't remember whose, or why she
                            came.
There are so many that I hardly care....
Heigh-ho – such are the penalties of
                                    fame!)
And if my sister's there, please will you
                                rescue us.
It doesn't do to be thought too incestuous!

And, Mrs P, when you have finished that,
Please could you wash the glasses and
                        the plate
And brush the carpet and shake out
                        the mat
(I hope it isn't in too bad a state!)
And, afterwards, oh, please put out
                        the cat,
(Or let it in if it has been out late)
And then wake me at noon with
                that which melts a
'Naching head – I mean a hock
                and seltzer!

From BARBARA CARTLAND'S WASTEPAPER BASKET

Sue Love,
Could you type this one
for me this morning?
Barbara.

THE WILD SHORES OF THE HEART

Pp.1-15	LOVE AT SECOND SIGHT
Pp.15-41	THE HEART HAS ITS SECRETS
Pp.42-67	STRANGERS IN LOVE
Pp.68-89	LOVE AT SECOND SIGHT
Pp.90-117	PASSIONATE SECRETS
Pp.118-136	STRANGERS IN LOVE
Pp.137-148	THE ROSE AND THE THORNS
Pp.149-157	LOVE AT SECOND SIGHT
Pp.158-170	FORGET-ME-NOT LOVE
Pp.171-186	STRANGERS IN LOVE

Change man's name throughout to "BRENT ROBERTS", girl's name throughout to "DAVINA CARSTAIRS", and name of other girl she thinks he's gone off with to "JOANNA KINGSTONE". Make setting CRETE - i.e. all inns called tavernas, local barman called Costas, swimming instead of tennis, Morning Glory instead of chrysanthemums, bit where he gets fresh and she says "No" on beach rather than in forest, a lot of pink in the sunsets, etc.

Franco 50 copies of this please

Oh My Darling

You are the only Woman for me. Since I met you, I have thought of nothing else.

I see other women, but they mean Nothing to me I will know no Peace until I possess you fully, and can show you with my Body, how much I Love You

Please, please make it possible

I will be in torment until I hear from you

Every last drop of My Love

Your Own

Giovanni

THINGS TO ~~DO~~ IN MUNICH.

1. TALK TO HERR HITLER
2. BUY SOME CHOCOLATE
3. ~~DON'T~~ LOSE THIS PIECE OF PAPER.

in a voice you could have scoured a soup pan with.

"Marlowe," I said. "Philip Marlowe."

The girl giggled with private merriment. Her lashes caressed her cheeks. She was neatly put together, and had been told so many times. She wore a navy-blue business suit with creases sharp enough to cut salami real thin. Her dark eyes were cold but looked as if they might come to the boil if the right flame was lit under them.

The man's eyes didn't look as if they'd heat up in a blast-furnace. He was about six feet four with none of it wasted in fat or compassion. The grey flannel suit he wore looked like it was having trouble holding him in. I got the feeling it wasn't only suits that'd have that problem.

"O.K., Mr. Marlowe. So what's your business?"

I said nothing. I let out a little cloud of cigarette smoke and watched it melt in the rather dim light of the office.

"I asked you a question," said the man.

I sank my lower jaw down on to my chest. "I'm thinking about an answer."

The girl liked that. She seemed to like seeing her boss cut down to size. I got the feeling doing a lot of that could be the way to bring her dark eyes to the boil. I also got the feeling it could be the way to get dead.

A flash from the man's eyes stopped her giggle before it dared come out.

"Listen, Marlowe. I don't have a lot of time. Don't fool around. Tell me why you're here."

I put one of my cards with the tommy gun in the corner on his desk. He looked at it as if I'd shoved last week's cheese sandwich up his nose.

"So you're a private detective. What's that to me?"

It was time to hit him with the facts. "I've been hired by Darnley Bombeck to find his daughter."

The facts hurt when they hit him. He gave me a look which ought to have made an exit-wound somewhere round the small of my back. He tried to recover himself, but didn't make up nearly enough ground.

"Why you telling me this, Mr. Marlowe?"

I blew a lungful of cigarette smoke at him. Maybe he'd never liked the taste, or if he had he'd gone off it.

I said: "I thought you might be interested."

He stared at me for a second or two. Then he said sharply: "As a private detective, what do you charge?"

"A hundred down as retainer — that's when I'm working with strangers. Then twenty-five a day, plus expenses."

"That include the car?"

"Eight cents a mile."

He nodded, his heavy jaw brushing against his powder-blue tie. "That's not a lot," he said in a thinking kind of voice.

I shrugged. The girl ran her fingers through her hair. She did it as if she'd rather someone else was doing it for her.

"Look, Marlowe," the man said. "I'd pay a lot more than that for you not to find Bombeck's daughter." I said nothing. "A thousand dollars?"

He let it hang in the air like bait. I shook my head. "Sorry. You got the wrong man."

"Two thousand dollars."

"Ah," I said. "Now you're talking. Give me the

Ye Tabard Inn
Southwerke
2 Aprile 1380

Dear Myster Chaucer
                Thisse is confirme
oore agremente thatte that thou
shalt have creditte withouten limitte
at ye Inne in exchange for wrytyne
a few lines of poesie to advertise
its vertues.

                            Please say
how goode a hostelrye ye Tabard be,
and how handye in Southwerk for
folk that wolde wenden on Pilgrimage
Saye also thatte we have beddes
for a compaignye of uppe to nyne and
twenty, that the chambers and the
stables area wyde, and that everich a
man or wooman that comes heere
Shall be esed atte beste. Saye thatte
it sneweth in this hous of mete and
drinke (at verye faire pryces)
        Enythynge else tho wishest to adde
to ye verses J leve to thy discresioun
but make Soore tho gettest inne ye
above pointes.
                    Yores ryghte Synceerely
                    J. Smythe
                            Myne Hoste.

Bath March 17 1748

Dear Boy

I must, from time to time, remind you of what I have often advised to you, and of what you cannot pay too much heed; decorum in relation to the touc:ung of the orifices of the body. The effects, in company, of the performance of these offices, is almost inconceivable. They infallibly give rise to disgust and, from your own observation, reflect how disgust, at first sight, prejudices you against a stranger, even when, for aught you know, he may be a man of great, though unseen, parts and merit.

A thousand little things, not all to be defined, conspire to generate this disgust, this je ne sais quoi, that cannot fail but offend. A pretty person, genteel motions, a proper degree of dress, an harmonious and properly varied manner of speaking: all these things, and many others, will be valued as naught in the man observed in society to pick his nose. Frequent and consistent continuation of the practise is the characteristic of folly and ill manners; it is the manner of the mob; and, as such, to be eschewed by a gentleman of the first quality.

Particularly to be guarded against is the trick of picking the nose, extracting therefrom its noxious effluvium, rolling this into balls, and either feeding these into the mouth, or flicking them with the fingers at members of the company. This very disagreeable habit is the characteristic of a natural fool, and a sure sign of futility.

No more to be recommended is the practice of putting the fingers to the ear and forming comparable rotundities from the waxen contents thereof. You cannot take too much pains, nor employ too much of your time in the avoidance of this, a habit which inevitably demonstrates the difference between minds cultivated and minds uncultivated.

Another evidence of ill-breeding and _mauvaise honte_, regrettably all too often seen in the salons of Europe, is scratching at the buttocks. Monsieur de Rochefoucault, in his Maxims, observes, that _il est plus facile de paraître comfortable sans culottes que le faire sans fesses_ a consideration greatly to be valued and respected, by those that may be called, in the common acceptation of the phrase, people of the first quality. Though no man, be he a person of quality or of the mob, may ever be immune from occasional discomfort of the fundament, attempts to alleviate this natural condition by friction must be the object of universal condemnation. A gentleman will rather bear with fortitude an infinity of tickling, than give way to the contemptible impulse to seek the relief of a scratching finger; a habit which can only degrade, vilify, and sink those who practise it, can only obstruct their rising in society, by debasing their reputations; and give them a low turn of mind and manners, absolutely inconsistent with their making any figure in upper life, or forming beneficial relationships at any relevant level of society.

Adieu, my dear child. Consider seriously the importance of what I have here advised you; and do not be diverted from your own advantage and final improvement by idle dissipations, low seduction, bad example, or buttock scratching.

This is

The Last Will and Testament

of me   AGATHA CHRISTIE

~~CANCELLED~~

I give and bequeath all ~~of~~ my estate and the ~~royalties for fifty~~ years after ~~my death~~ unto ~~my loving~~ ~~most~~ nephew, Eric, from Australia, unless he dies within a month of my death, in which case ~~the~~ property shall go to his illegitimate brother, Henry, ~~the~~ ~~solicitor~~. If, however, both brothers die within a month of my death, the beneficiary of this will shall be ~~my~~ housekeeper, Winifred Caistor, who is really the daughter ~~of~~ my doctor, Marmaduke Dollington. In the event of Winifred dying within a month of my death, her ~~father~~ will inherit, but only if he is reconciled with his estranged wife, Daphne. If, however, Daphne dies before the month is up, the police should be called and, after Marmaduke's arrest, my estate should go to his niece, my long suffering nurse, Betty. Should Betty die in suspicious circumstances

In Xanadu did Kubla Khan
Have to be a right Don Juan
He had Khartel knowledge
Of nine girls from college
And ~~staggered~~ ten ~~asleep~~ in
a barn.

It's no good! Since that
person came on business from
Porlock, I just can't get
back into the idiom of it!

From E.E. CUMMINGS'S WASTEPAPER BASKET

ACME
TYPEWRITER COMPANY

Sales, Service and Repairs

17th August, 1919

Dear Mr. Cummings,

We have examined the typewriter you left with us yesterday, and regret that we are unable to repair the defective "Shift" key.

May we recommend to your attention our latest model, the TITAN, which retails at a mere S147.50, and would be ideal for a working poet like yourself.

Looking forward to hearing from you,

Yours sincerely,

G. Liebermann

SALES MANAGER

you know nothing's happened
and I know nothing's happened
[and nothings going to happen
— got that, sonny?] but who's
going to believe that when
you go on writing all this
stuff?

So, for the last time, I
ask you — will you bloody
well stop it! get off my
back! I dare say there are
plenty of girls around who
wouldn't mind inspiring you,
but you've got the wrong
one with me — understand?

so stop writing
about me!!

Beatrice

From CHARLES DICKENS'S WASTEPAPER BASKET

(Because of the condition of the manuscript it has been impossible to reproduce the original, and this is a transcription of the text.)

THE MYSTERY OF EDWIN DROOD

CHAPTER 23

The Veiled Lady

London. Summer still choking the city breathless. Summer mixing dust with the smoke spilling down from chimney pots. Summer adding the shimmer of heat-haze to this clogging compound of dust and smoke, stirring a witches' brew of bright opacity, veiling, fragmenting and trembling the vistas of towers and terraces, corner shops and cathedrals, bridges and barges, tobacconists and tenements. Summer breaking the images of the city into slivers of coloured glass, changing the picture with the twist of a wrist, like some giant child's hand, experimenting on Christmas morning with its newly-unwrapped kaleidoscope.

Dust everywhere. Dust making tiny archipelagoes on the surface of cold water in bedroom bowls. Dust dulling the shine of tables and cabinets, tall-boys and cake-stands, coffers and closets. Dust in the kitchens, mocking the cooks' mania for cleanliness; dust in the drawing-rooms, caught as slow-moving motes by the diagonals of morning sunlight, biding their time, spinning gently, abstracted, selecting the destinations on which they will descend. Dust in the eyes and ears and throats of the waking world; dust tickling at early morning mouths, calling out the coughs with the peremptory despatch of an usher in a court-room. Dust also summoning up from their cells a dirty company of spits, hawks and hacks.

And dust stirred by the hem of the dress of the veiled lady who walks the early morning streets from the docks towards a hybrid hotel at the dingy end of Cheesemaker Street. Her veil adds another distortion to the refractions of the dust, and London looms, ominous and lowering, like a land seen in a dream, through the unfamiliar net which curtains her face. Her clothes, too, the heavy swatches of cloth across her shoulders, the long swish of skirts against the ground, all feel strange. She seems a creature from the land of dreams, swimming on the surface of the heat-haze.

That behind the veil the lady is thinking, and that the thoughts of one recently arrived from foreign shores must be vivid, is not to be doubted. But can we know the nature of her thoughts? Do they run on John Jasper? Is Mr. Grewgious allowed access to the private rooms of her mind? Does Mr. Crisparkle loll about there, making himself at home, perhaps sitting down in an armchair, with his slippered feet up on one of the mental tables of that secret place?

Alas, we cannot know; and even if we tried to read the mind's construction in the lady's face, we would be frustrated by the dark curtain of her veil.

If her face is denied to us, her hands may perhaps speak volumes of information. Are they the scarred hands of a serving-woman, the white hands of a lady? Do they bear encrustations of jewellery, are they legitimised by a wedding ring?

Alas, we cannot know; for as her face is shrouded by a

veil, so are her hands hidden by gloves of kid.

But let us follow her. Yes, perhaps if we follow her through the dusty doorway of her sad hotel, we may be allowed to share a little of her secret. To the clerk she goes, a moping, fat boy, hardly awake; with almost masculine imperatives, she commands a room. Her travelling baggage will be coming in a fly from the docks; she gives the fat boy instructions for its disposition. Wheezing a little, he leads her up the dusty stairs to a little dusty room. This she surveys, noting with approval the dusty window that looks out on nothing more than an eyeless, dusty wall; and, pressing a half-crown into the damp, dusty hand, tells the fat boy it will serve.

She waits diligently till the descending footsteps have melted to silence, and the fat boy can be presumed to have resubmerged in the torpor from whence she stirred him; then she moves towards the room's one, dusty, mirror. She reaches with one large kid-gloved hand to release the buttons of the other.

Now what will we see? Now will we be granted fragments of the veiled lady's secret? The hands from which the gloves are withdrawn are brown - not the brown of the Brahmin or the African, but the brown of the European unsheltered from a foreign sun. Where have her hands been to return so stained? The curious ring she wears (not on the wedding finger) may tell us. Yes, it is North African work; the beaten silver whorls murmur softly to us the word: "Morocco".

Enough of the hands. They have performed their small betrayal and told us all they know. But still they can help us, as they move up to detach the veil and reveal a new informer, the lady's face. It is a sad face they unshroud, a face of suffering; it is a face, too, that, in some way not to be defined, is familiar to us. It is a face that has known pain - not only the distant pains of adversity, but also the more recent pains of...what? Is it illness? Not quite. No, it is a face that has recently suffered the pains of the surgeon's knife.

But can we know why the scalpel, saw and knife were needed? Surely, we insist, it must have been an illness that laid the veiled lady low? Her face denies that; it is too robust, too strong. Her face seems to whisper that, whatever operation she has so recently suffered, it was undertaken voluntarily.

The strangeness of these messages confuses us. Can we ever solve this conundrum, sort out the bizarre contradictions of the information the hands and face have confessed to us? Without more help, I fear not.

But, even as we think this, arrives that help, like a refreshing breeze lifting the dust of this hot, dusty day. The lady speaks, at once untangling the muddled skeins of our conjecture. She looks at her heavy-browed eyes in the dusty mirror, and, with a smile like an evening shadow stealing across her face, murmurs, "Welcome back to England, Edwina Drood."

THE STRAND MAGAZINE

5 February 1886

Dear Dr Doyle,

Many thanks for submitting your short story, which I feel shows great promise. The idea of solving crimes by deduction is an excellent one.

My only quibble though ~~choice of hero. Dr Watson~~ is clearly an intelligent ~~man with~~ He is also a compassionate one (as we see in his treatment of the arrogant dope-fiend Sherlock Holmes), but I'm afraid, in spite of his deductive brilliance, he does come across as rather boring.

So, regretfully, I return your manuscript herewith. Please don't be discouraged. I feel sure that with some very simple changes, the story could work.

Yours Sincerely

JG Pennsum

Editor

Lloyds Bank

17, Cornhill,
London E.C.

13th November 1917.

Dear Mr. Prufrock,
                    Banking folk
Cannot show very much sympathy,
And your statement is spread out over my desk
Like a body in its shroud upon a table.

You have measured out your life with apologies,
But there comes a time
Between time future and time past,
Which should perhaps be called time present,
When the bank can no longer honour your overdraft.

That is a way of putting it - not wholly satisfactory:
A maybe tactless statement
Of the tired-out financial cliché
"This bank is not a charitable institution",
Not a place
Where hopes can be extended infinitely,
Month by month.

And October was your most extravagant month, spending
Money that was not yours, raising
Borrowings and credit, making
Bad debts with this bank.

I observe, from your letter,
That you have had unexpected failures
Which have turned your sales-graph downwards,
But that you hope to turn again
You hope to turn.

Do not forget,
I am aware that this sort of thing has occured before.
For you each venture
Is a new beginning, a new promise of future prosperity.

I know you, though,
Full of high speeches, but a bit unsure;
At times, indeed, downright dishonest.

Between your promise
And the reality
Between your intention
And the act
Comes the Excuse

I know what you are thinking-
That all we bank clerks come and go
Talking of flow and counterflow.
That
We are the heartless men
We are the stuffed shirts
Grinning together.

But, Mr. Prufrock,
Think of me as you must,
A dry old man,
Wearing a young man's trousers,
(Though I have known the anguish of the miser,
The agony of the spendthrift),
But you do not wish to know
Do not wish to know
My problems.

DO NOT ATTEMPT
DO NOT ATTEMPT TO CASH
DO NOT ATTEMPT TO CASH ANY FURTHER CHEQUES.
Or Sosostris and Eugenides,
Our solicitors,
Will be in touch.

Yours
Sincerely. Sincerely.
        Sincerely   sincerely   sincerely

        T.S. ELIOT

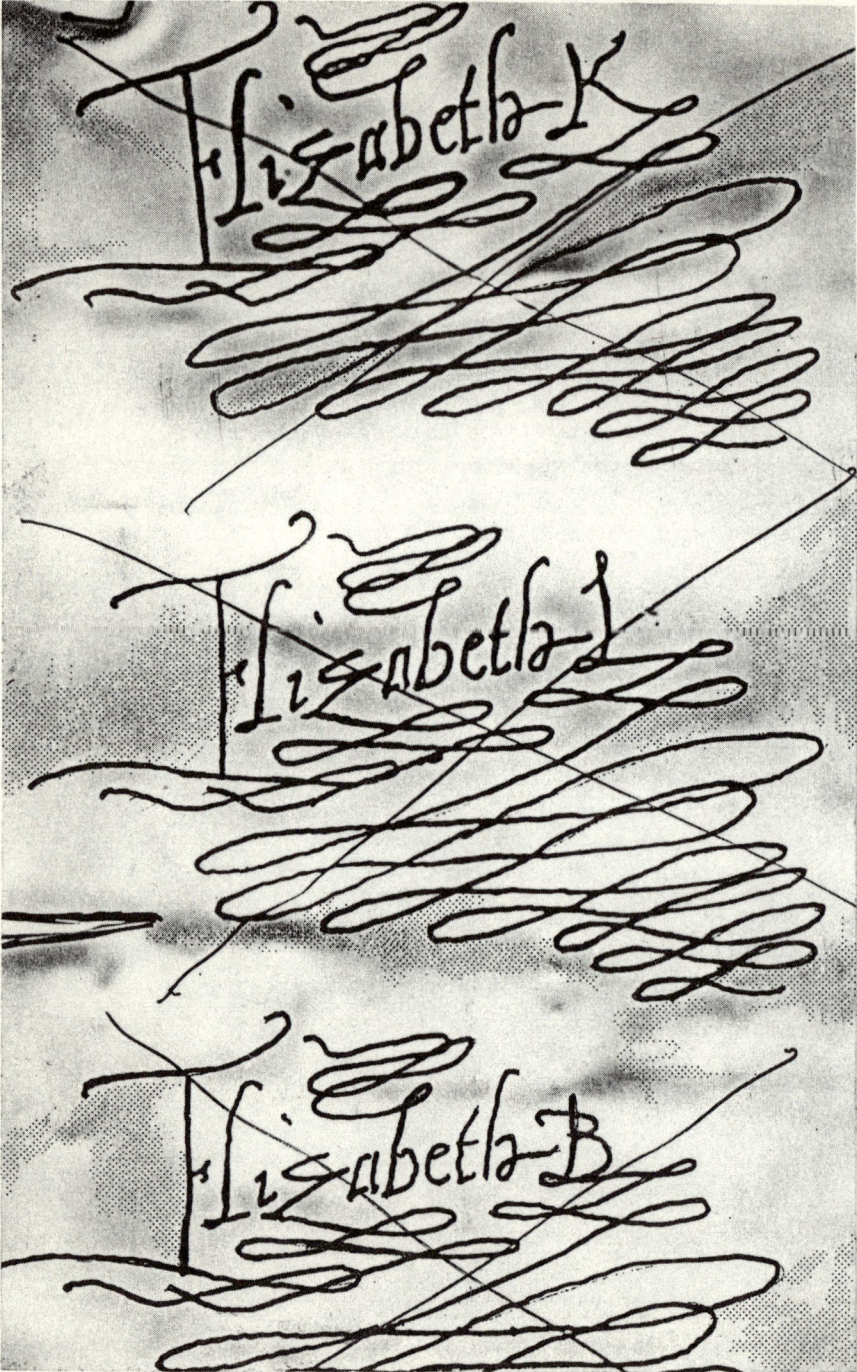

From BARON VON FRANKENSTEIN'S WASTEPAPER BASKET

transyl electricity

ENQUIRIES TO:

GALVANITE HOUSE,
TRANSYLVANIA.

TO PAY, SEE OVER

FINAL NOTICE

BARON VON FRANKENSTEIN,
CASTLE FRANKENSTEIN,
VLADBURG,
TRANSYLVANIA.

QUOTE this REFERENCE NUMBER

3414 093 073 002

Normal reading date

20 OCT 82

V.A.T Registration No. 228 5879 21. No V.A.T. is shown on this account as all charges for 'electricity' are ZERO RATED.

PREVIOUS READING	PRESENT READING	TARIFF	UNITS	PENCE PER UNIT	AMOUNT £ p
3	98769353213	DOMESTIC	765329721	4.8	45768594322 17
QUARTERLY CHARGE					7 28
		TOTAL NOW DUE			45768594329 45

The amount shown above still appears to be outstanding. Should the account have been paid within the past few days, please disregard this notice and accept our apologies for reminding you of the matter again.

If the amount has not been paid, and payment in full is not received within seven days, the account will be referred to the appropriate department for the issue of legal proceedings and this could involve you in the additional cost of court fees.

C against a meter reading indicates it is your own reading
E indicates an estimate. Any under or over estimates will be corrected at the next meter reading

Payment is now due

TO : The W~~o~~manager,   17th ~~Orgies~~ [August], 1904

    United Austrian ~~W~~[B]ank,

    32, ~~Tit~~[Tetel]sstrasse,

    VIENNA.

Dear Her~~r~~ Kuntz~~l~~er,

    I must apologise for the current state of my ~~potency~~ [account]. I see from your recent ~~French~~ letter that I am 23,734 Schillings over~~sexed~~ [drawn], and I very much regret ~~seeing my parents copulating.~~ [this oversight]

    I can assure you that there is ~~everything~~ [nothing] to worry about. I know that the size of my ~~penis~~ [overdraft] is currently larger than the facility we agreed, but I hope very soon to be able to make ~~love to my mother~~ [up the deficit]. Within the next week I will be paying in the proceeds of the sale of some g~~y~~ilt-edged security bonds ~~and manacles and whips~~. I am also owed considerable sums of money by clients for my ~~sexual~~ [psychiatric] services.

    Until those payments have ~~come into~~ [come into] my account, I will endeavour not to make any further ~~withdrawals~~ [withdrawals].

    In the hope that you will ~~bare~~ [bear] with me for a little longer and extend the ~~full length of your willy~~ [limit of my agreed overdraft facility] for another month.

              ~~Whores~~ [Yours] sincerely,

              S~~U~~[IG]CKMUND FRA~~I~~[EU]D

Well, Mr Windy wasn't going to stand for that.

"No, Mr. Nosey," he said. "I'm not going to stand for that."

"OH NO?" said Mr Nosey.

"NO!" said Mr Windy.

And then he let fly a REALLY BIG ONE.

Poor Mr. Nosey!

They were sitting in a restaurant in the Bois. They had had a good dinner. They had had good wine. It was a good party.

I walked in. "Hey," Brad said. "You having a good time? We're having a good time."

I rubbed my forehead. "Not such a good time."

"I heard your head was bad," Nick said. "Heard it got bad in the war."

"The hell with the war. My mother says I always had these migraines. As a kid I had these migraines."

"Have another brandy," the count said. No one answered. They all wanted more brandy. "Bud?"

"Hell, no," I said. "I don't drink. Plays hell with my digestion."

"Lots of people lost a lot in the war," Nick said. "Some lost more than digestion."

"Not the war. My mother says my digestion was bad when I was a kid. Nerves."

They were quiet.

"Anyway," I said, "drinking alcohol doesn't do you any good. Makes grown men do damnfool things, like kids."

They stayed quiet. A nigger singer started. People danced.

"Dance, Bud?" Martha said. "I need to dance."

Martha was damn good-looking. She was built with the curves of a hunting rifle, and she knew it. She was a tall girl who sat still with a great deal of movement.

"Dance?" I said. "No, I don't dance."

"Come on, dance. Everyone's dancing."

"I know. I personally don't dance."

"Hell, dance."

"No. My mother knew a young man who gotten fallen arches from dancing."

Martha danced with Brad. He was a good dancer, but not a great dancer. The nigger singer waved at Martha. She spat at him.

Their glasses were empty. They asked the waiter for more _fines_. I asked him for mineral water, regular mineral water, not the gassy mineral water that I drank with Miguel on the Aguilado the time he tried to get me interested in fishing, and couldn't. That mineral water gave me wind. The waiter brought regular mineral water. I drank it. It was good.

"You see the fight?" the count said. "It was a good fight."

"Fight?"

"Lacompte-Frank Martin. He can box, Martin."

"Box?"

"You see the fight?"

"No, I didn't see the fight. I don't see fights. I don't like fights. My mother says boxing appeals to man's lowest instincts."

"Sure," said Nick. "What's wrong with man's lowest instincts?"

I was silent, not silent with the silence of someone who hasn't got anything to say, but silent with the silence of someone making someone else think about what they just said. My mother used to use that kind of silence a lot. Nick thought about what he just said. He was silent.

The music stopped. The nigger singer waved at Martha again. She slapped him. Martha and Brad came over to the table. Martha sat down. So did Brad.

"We had a good time," Brad said.

"We had a good time?" Martha said.

"You're a lovely piece."

Martha slapped Brad. She pulled the felt hat down far over her nose.

The glasses were empty. The waiter brought more _fines_. Martha changed from brandy to pernod. I had more mineral water. It was good, but not as good as the first time.

"Next week they are running the bulls in Pamplona," Nick said.

"Bulls?"

The count smiled. For him the bulls were a special secret, a secret some people would not understand. I knew all about the secret. I was one of the people who did not understand it.

"Will you run with the bulls?" he asked Brad.

Brad smiled. It was his secret, too. "I'll run."

"And if you get gored?" Martha said.

"I get gored. The hell with it, I get gored."

He ordered more drinks. He ordered pernod for Martha. Martha hit him. She had changed from pernod to champagne. He ordered champagne for Martha. I had more mineral water. This time it was hardly good at all.

"You go to Pamplona, Bud? Run with the bulls?"

The music started again. The nigger singer smiled at Martha. She pulled out a gun and shot him. The music went on. People danced.

"Hell, no," I said. "I wouldn't do that for a bet. Bulls?" I wrinkled my nose. "Bull-fighting? Hell, you joking me? It's disgusting. And so cruel to the bulls. Dangerous, too. My mother says that bull-fighting is one of the most degrading and despicable forms of cruelty that human beings

Wolsey, I think this is a ryghte shytty idea 𝄞𝓗𝓡𝓗

Tudorwaye Datynge Servise
For Companyonshippe Casual Affaires and Marriage

please fille in ye followynge questionnaire

name *Henry* age — occupation *King*

religion *mine Owne* heighte *Great* girthe *massyve*

dost thou see thyselfe as

A	comely	aye/~~nay~~
B	sexy	aye/~~nay~~
C	confidente	aye/~~nay~~
D	basheful	~~aye~~/nay

what are thy interestes?

Women, hunting, eatynge, wrytynge, musicke.
executynge people who disagree with me
et cetera

what sorte of partner art thou lookynge for?

sexe *female* age *young* occupation *princesse or queen*

religion *mine* height *small* girthe *slender*

dost thou wishe thy partner to be

A	comely	aye/~~nay~~
B	sexey	aye/~~nay~~
C	riche	aye/~~nay~~
D	domesticated	~~aye~~/nay

an other special requirements?

Lette her be fertile to beare many sonnes!

what interestes dost thou wish thy partner to have? *none (save mine)*

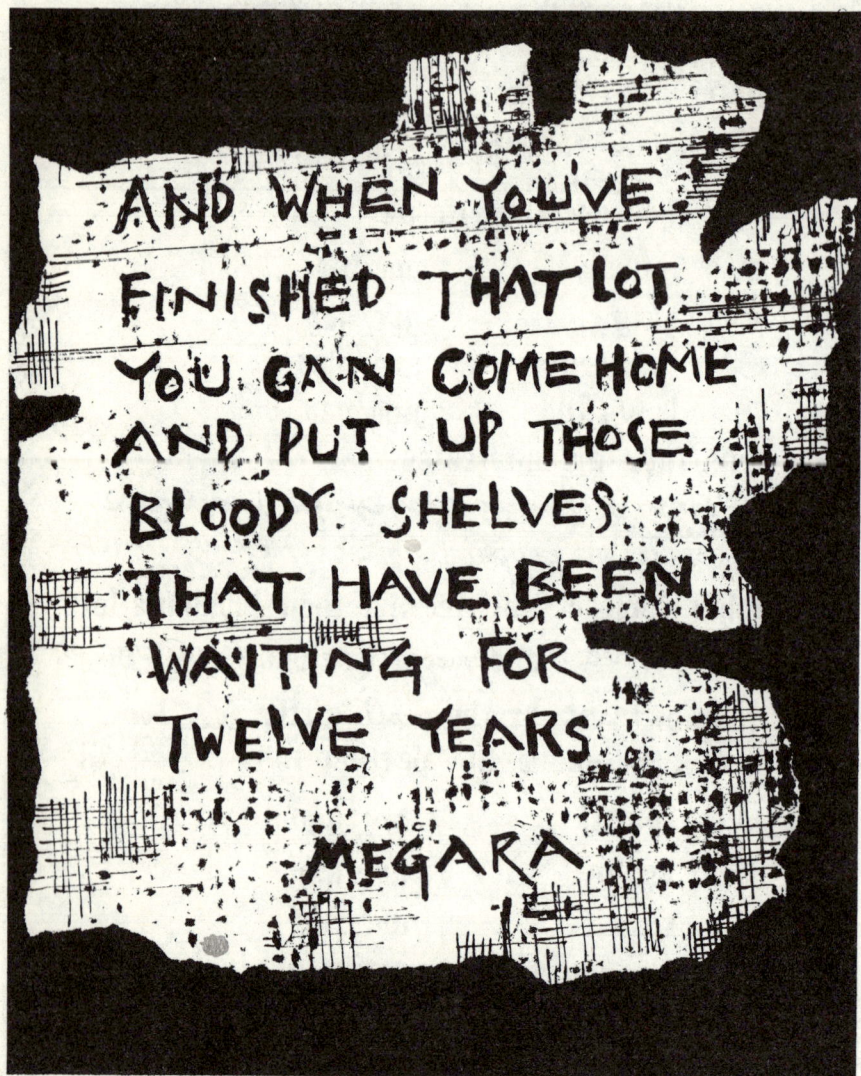

AND WHEN YOU'VE
FINISHED THAT LOT
YOU CAN COME HOME
AND PUT UP THOSE
BLOODY SHELVES
THAT HAVE BEEN
WAITING FOR
TWELVE YEARS
MEGARA

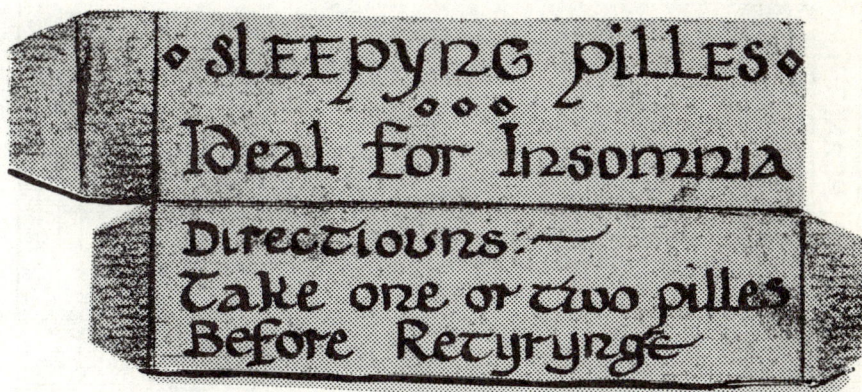

✠ 1940 YEAR PLANNER

SHOPPING LIST

I must this morning's morning shopping buy, stop-
    ping at grossest grocers; gather grainèd green
    bacon, not forgetting
    Half of red-wrapped Edam, and I'll get
      the cheddar there (all sweating
High there — how it stinks upon the blat of
      the shoddy shop —
Smell it putrefy!) Then off, off, buy a chop,
    And a cow's heel comes close on my
      long list. Then stakes and netting
    To box the big trees (and thus not letting
Herds of the birds to demolish, to nibble up
    all the crop).

Bread, biscuits and veal-chops and what ...?
    Oh, what? Buy booze, yes ...
    Baked beans! And that fish that flakes
      from the bone, and cereal ...
Quick cook porridge and ... more sausages!
    Oh, I'm in a mess!

No wonder of it: Shopping seems immaterial.
Some men can cope with chores. I confess
    I, I myself, I'm much more ethereal.

ON PRINCE WILLIAM LOSING
HIS FIRST BABY-TOOTH

Born out of blood, like a stain
Left where the hawk fells his prey,
The stripped red-raw sinew
Shows in the open mouth.

White, like a tiny vertebra
Severed from its spine,
The hard-gritted biter
Works free, and wobbles

Loose, riven from the jaw.
Spat, smoking, to the pillow,
Trailing its string of blood,
It rips out a baby-cry.

The small white stone saved,
Not for the offal-bin
But under-pillow returned
To await the Tooth Fairy.

DON'T WORRY YOU'RE NOT PARANOID WE REALLY ARE OUT TO GET YOU

Oh what can ail thee knight at arms
Alone and palely loitering;
The sedge is wither'd from the lake
And no birds sing.

Ah what can ail thee wretched wight,
So haggard and so woe-begone?
The squirrel's granary is full,
And the harvest's done.

I see a lilly on thy brow,
With anguish moist, and fever dew;
It looks to me that Benskin's Pills
Are the things for you.

Sorry Mr Keats I'm afraid I and the rest of the Marketing Department here at Benskins had visualised a more aggressive campaign. Hope you can do something with this.

J Thompson

just seems to me.
a rather elaborate way of
committing suicide, but you've
the President, so if that's
what you want, I can
certainly arrange it. There's
a guy called Lee Harvey
Oswald, who I reckon could
be just the sort of
you'll

What?

What? You can keep your
head when all ~~around~~ about you.
Are losing their's and ~~saying~~ blaming
~~it was~~ it on you.
What? You can trust yourself
when ~~everyone doubts~~ all men doubt you
~~But never mind about~~ make allowance
their doubting too
What? You can wait, and.

The Rt. Hon. Nigel Lawson, P.C., M.P.,
Chancellor of the Exchequer,
11, Downing Street,
London S.W.1.

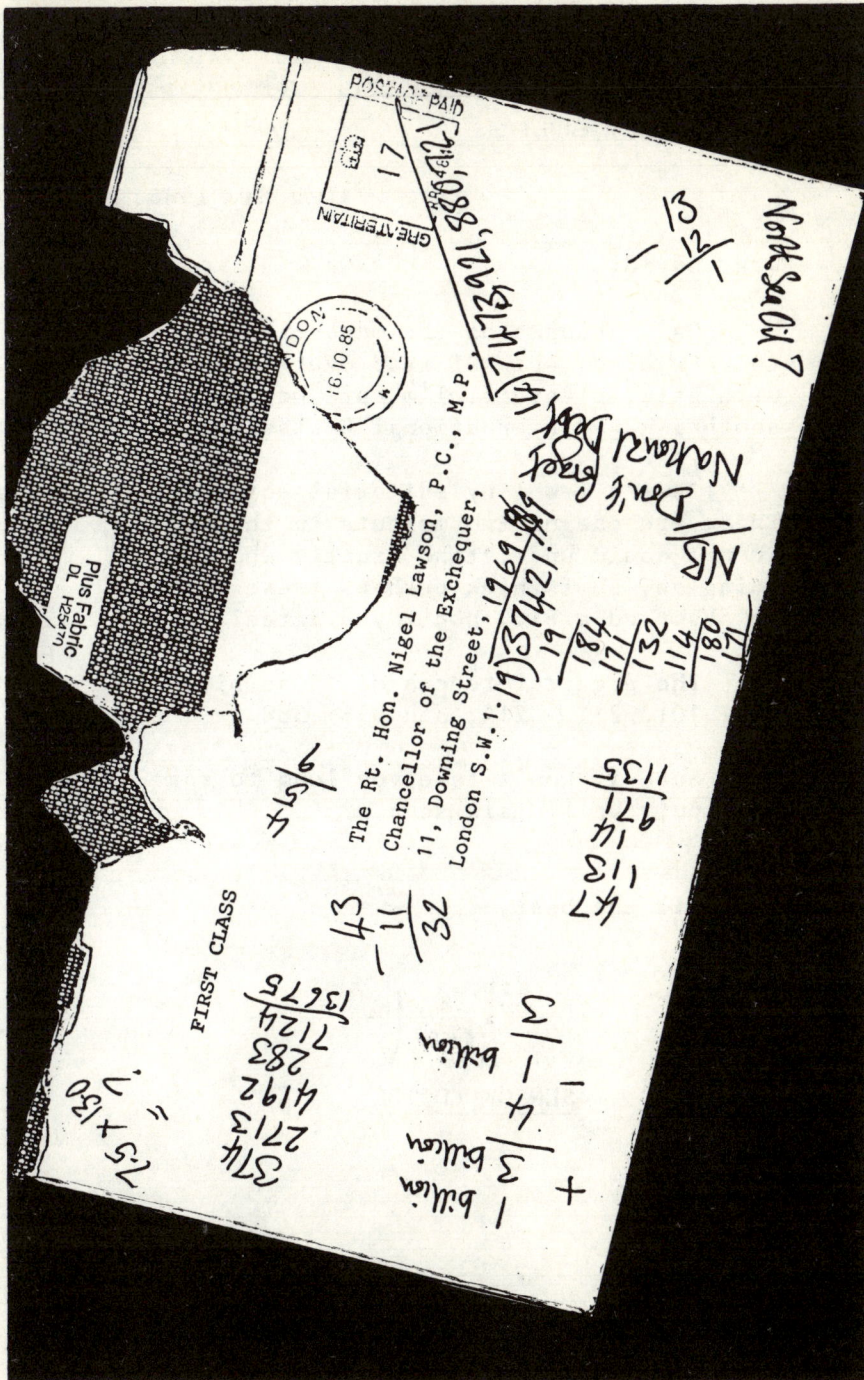

POSTAGE PAID
GREAT BRITAIN
17

LONDON
16.10.85

Plus Fabric
DL H25?tn

FIRST CLASS

North Sea Oil?

NB/ Don't forget National Debt

$\frac{13}{12}$
1

1-19(3)742'1;1769:84
$\frac{19}{184}$
$\frac{17}{132}$
$\frac{114}{180}$
17

$\frac{1135}{126}$
$\frac{14}{113}$
47

45/94

$\frac{43}{32}$
- 11

3714
2713
4192
283
$\frac{7124}{13675}$

75 × 130 = ?

- 1 billion + 1 billion
$\frac{3}{4}$
$\frac{1}{1}$
- 1 billion

HODDER & STOUGHTON LTD
BOOK PUBLISHERS

14th May 1986.

Dear David,

Many thanks for the manuscript of
the new book, which I read over the weekend
with great pleasure. I'm sure we're on to
another huge international bestseller.

Just a few tiny editorial points.
There are one or two moments in the book
when I could understand exactly what was
going on, so I think perhaps these should
be obscured a bit. Don't you agree?

The page references of these bits are
97 - 101, 211 - 214, and 378 -388.

Sure it won't take you long to sort
them out. We'll talk soon.

All the best,

Yours,

Nigel.

SENIOR EDITOR

ANGLO - SAXON CHRONICLE

10 December 1040

Dear Earl Leafric,

Thank you very much for sending me the tapestry of your wife, Lady Godiva, on horseback, and for your suggestion that it might look good on Page III of the "Chronicle". I regret, however, that this would be against the paper's editorial policy.

yours sincerly

Eagfrith Angelthieow

editor

P.S. I apologise that I am unable to return your tapestry herewith, but I'm afraid it seems to have got lost in the Newsroom

THE ETIQUETTE

OF THE TENNIS COURT

Tennis is a game played by gentlemen and ladies, and it is important that this is never forgotten in the conduct of a game. The sporting spirit behind all athletic endeavours is most important in tennis, and at no time should standards of behaviour be allowed to slip.

The first point, which should hardly need making, is that there should be no cheating. The rules of tennis have evolved over a long period and are perfectly adequate to the demands placed upon them. In the final analysis, when there is any dispute, it should be referred in a calm and dignified manner to the umpire. And when the umpire's ruling on the matter is given, that is the end of the argument. Under no circumstances should the decision of the umpire be questioned. Experienced players of the game know that the proper

127

The Tay Bridge Disaster

Oh, beautiful Bridge o'er the Silvery Tay!
Alas! Oh, how great is my sorrow to say
That ninety brave lives have been taken away
On the very last Sunday of '79,
Which will not be forgotten in God's great design

'Twas seven o'clock on that doom-laden night
And the wind was a-blowing with all its might,
And the merciless rain came a-guttering down,
And the lowering clouds seemed to threaten & frown,
And the Demon of Air seem'd to bluster and say—
"I'll blow down the Bridge on the Silvery Tay."

When the train started out from down Edinburgh way
The passengers all felt quite bonny and gay,
But Boreas then blew a terrible gale,
Which made all their hearts and their spirits to quail,
And made all the passengers fearfully say,
"May God send us safely right over the Tay."

The train was arriving just near Hermit Bay,
When Boreas angrily started to bray
And shook all the girders on that
Bridge of Tay.
On the very last Sunday of '79
Which will long be remembered—

No Sod it, This isn't Working!

AND I CAN GAURANTEE THAT YOULL NEVER HAVE SEEN ANYTHING LIKE IT AND WHEN IT'S FULLY EXTENDED IT'S AT LEAST <u>18 INCHES</u> LONG — AND IF YOU DON'T BELIEVE ME COME ROUND TO MY PLACE AND <u>MEASURE IT</u>.!! I'm IN MOST EVENINGS AFTER SIX AND YOU WOULDN'T BE "WASTING YOUR TIME" IF YOU <u>CAME</u> ROUND! I HAVEN'T <u>COME ACROSS</u> ANYONE WHO'S SEEN ONE LIKE IT.!! THOUGH I'VE MET A FEW PEOPLE WHO <u>WISH THAT THERES WAS HALFAS</u>

14th August 1967

Dear Jonathan,

I was, needless to say, very disappointed to hear that you have irrevocably decided to give up the theatre for medicine. I know it must be your decision.

26 Nov. 1974.

Mr Miller

I am so sorry that you have ...ded to give up your medical work in favour of the theatre. All of us at the hospital

7th May, 1977

Jonathan,

So medicine has finally won out, has it? Well, I can't say I'm surprised, though, of course, you will be much missed in the theatre and your many frie... I'm sure, w...

19th March, 1979

...iller,

All of us in the Research Unit were saddened to hear that you have decided finally to give up medicine in favour of the theatre. Needless to say, ...ny research project needs time before it ...hieves results and we are sorry that ...following ...ch I feel we ...

...and can fully understand the reaso... you want to give up the theatre and con... ...ate on medicine. After all, it's 1982, we... us getting any younger and if yo... ...do... ...ore for the benefit...

26th November, 1985

Dear Dr. Miller,

So, you have decided that medicine is not for you, after all, and are going back to work in the theatre. None of us can pretend that we share your sense of priorities, but we all hope sincerely that you will not reg... decision an...

PARADISE LOST
BOOK ONE

Of mans first disobedience, and the fruit
Of that forbidden tree, whose mortal shoot
Brought death into the world, and all our fate
With loss of Eden, till one Man more great
Restore us, and regain the bliss we seek,
Sing, heavenly Muse, that on the secret peak
Of Oreb, or of Sinai, didst exhort
That shepherd, who the chosen seed first taught
In the beginning how the heavens and ground
Rose out of chaos: or if Sion's mound
Delight thee more, and Siloa's brook that ran
Fast by the oracle of God; I can
Invoke thy aid to my adventurous lay
That with no middle flight intends to stay
Above the Aonian mount, but aims to climb
Heights unattempted yet in English rhyme

XI. THOU SHALT NOT BE SMUG
IF THOU RECKONEST THOU
HAST KEPT ALL THE OTHER
TEN

XII. THOU SHALT NOT GO TO
CHURCH UNLESS IT MEANETH
SOMETHING UNTO TO THEE

XIII. THOU SHALT NOT EVER SAY
"WOMEN ALWAYS MEAN YES
WHEN THEY SAY NO"

XIV. THOU SHALT NOT SELL
INSURANCE

XV. THOU SHALT GIVE THE
BENEFIT OF THE DOUBT
UNTO ALL (EXCEPT OF
COURSE UNTO THEY THAT
DO SELL INSURANCE)

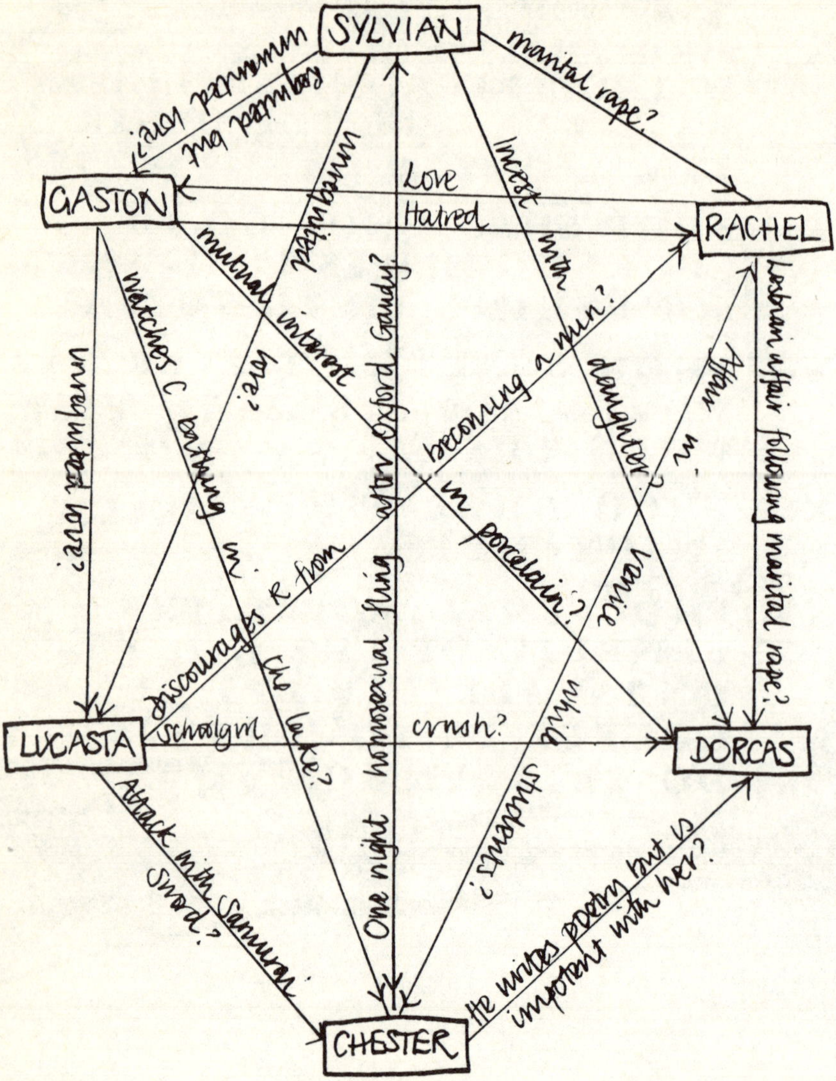
SYLVIAN
GASTON
RACHEL
LUCASTA
DORCAS
CHESTER
marital rape?
regarded but
unrequited love?
unrequited love?
Love
Hatred
Incest with daughter?
Lesbian affair following marital rape?
mutual interest in porcelain?
watches C bathing in the lake?
One night homosexual fling after Oxford Gaudy?
discourages R from becoming a nun?
Affair in Venice while student?
unrequited love?
schoolgirl crush?
Attack with Samurai sword?
He writes poetry but is impotent with her?

FAC MVSICAM VIOLINAE IN
VII DIES

AB

LABIENVS MINIMVS

AVCTOR — "FACILITAS TVBAE"
"TYMPANVM PRO TIRO CVM
LABIENVS"

LYRAM CANERE AB INITIO

ET CETERA, ET CETERA....

DOCVMENTVM PRIMVM :

MVSICA DOMI BELLA EST. MEHERCLE, VIR
QVIS MVSICAM NESCIT, IMBECILLIS EST. SED VIR
QVIS MVSICAM FACERE SCIT, NON SOLVS AD
OPTIMA CONVIVIA INVITATATVS EST SED ETIAM
CVM PVELLAE PROSPERIT. ERGO, MVSICA DISCERE
BONA NOTIO EST. ET, MVLTORVM INTRVMENTORVM
QVAM IN EMPORIA EMPTANDA SVNT, VIOLINA
BELLISIMA EST, FACILIS QVOQVE PROPTER MODI
OPERANDI SIMPLICITATEM. DIGITVS EST

At the Close there's a
      breathless hush tonight —
Eight to make & the game
            to win —
A failing pitch and a fading
            light,
One more hour and the last
            man's in.
But since all you'll get is
      a ribbon'd coat,
Or the worthless hope of a
      season's fame,
Tell the Captain you're off
      to have a smoke —
"Give up! give up! and
   stuff the game!"

Beaucoup de gens vont lire ce quatrain,
Quand trois cent ans sont certainement passés :
Ils auront tous une livre à la main :
L'archive de la Corbeille aux papiers

[An approximate translation of this prophecy
would run as follows :
  " Many people will read these four lines
    When at least three hundred years have gone by.
    They will all be holding a book called
    ' The Wastepaper Basket Archive '."]

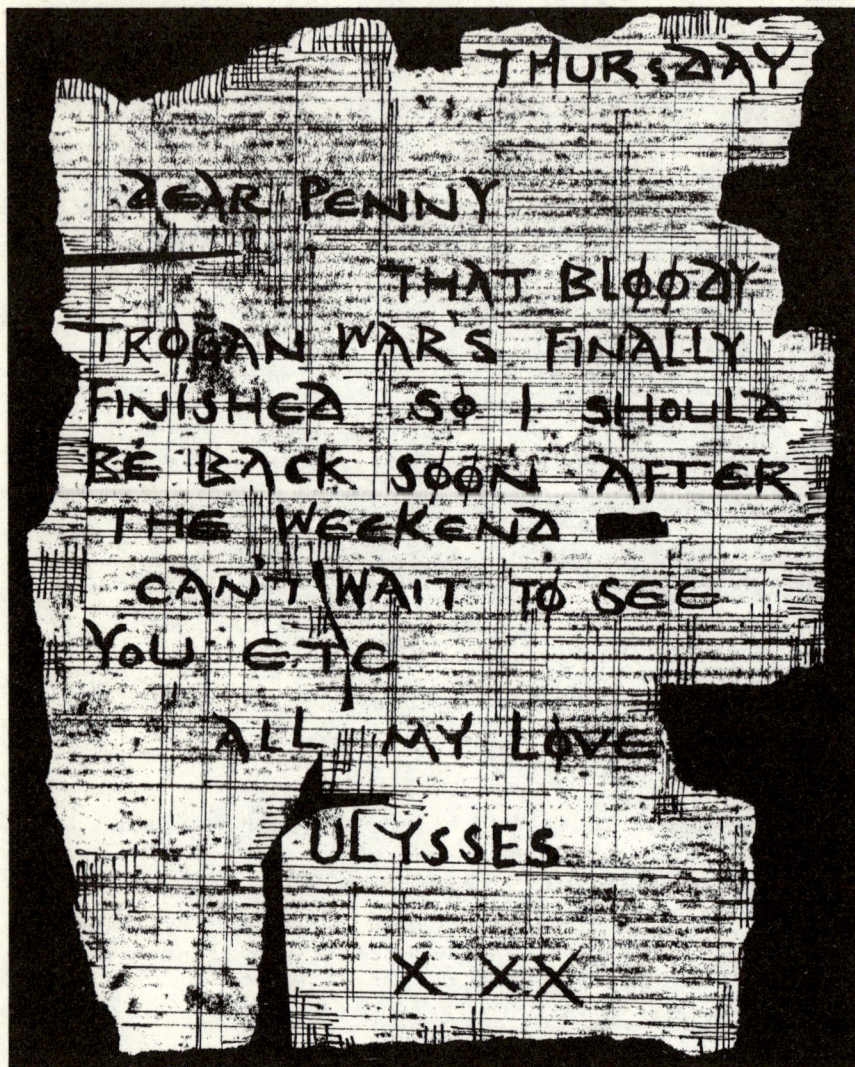

THURSDAY

DEAR PENNY

THAT BLOODY
TROJAN WAR'S FINALLY
FINISHED SO I SHOULD
BE BACK SOON AFTER
THE WEEKEND
CAN'T WAIT TO SEE
YOU ETC
ALL MY LOVE

ULYSSES

X XX

SALVADOR RODRIGUES
Optician & Lensmaker ⊙⊙

Avenida Cervantes 235, Barcelona.

23 de octubre de 1904.

Dear Senor Picasso,

    We have recently been checking our records, and discovered that, when you ordered spectacles from us four years ago, you were unfortunately given the wrong prescription, and received a pair of blue-tinted glasses prepared for another customer.

    We apologise deeply for this mistake, which can be rectified immediately, and hope that it has not caused you any inconvenience.

    With profuse apologies,

      Yours sincerely,

[signature]

MANAGER

From HAROLD PINTER'S WASTEPAPER BASKET

ASTON : So? ~~What you don't realise is that the number on the door of this room is Six, but the screw has fallen out of the top of the plastic numeral and~~ (PAUSE) ~~and it's dropped down so that it now looks like a~~ Nine!

DAVIES : ~~Nine! Oh no! You realise what this means? It means that~~ when my girl-friend Fifi Ladouche comes along ~~for our secret~~ assignation at three o'clock, there's a strong chance that she'll not be able to find ~~the~~ room. I distinctly told her Number Six, but if it says Nine on the door...she might be put off. ~~Oh crikey!~~ That could really put the ~~lid on things~~ ~~look, we must work out a plan to stop a disaster from happening.~~ What do you say? (PAUSE) ~~Well, come on - what do you say?~~

ASTON : ~~I see your problem. I know you've been looking forward to a naughty couple of hours with Fifi ever since you met her at that conference in Brighton. And the way things are turning out this afternoon, you know what it looks as if you're going to get for all your hard work and careful planning?~~ Nothing. (PAUSE) ~~Oh crikey! I forgot to tell you. There was a message at reception from your wife.~~ She said to tell you she would be arriving here at three o'clock.

DAVIES : ~~My wife! Here! At three o'clock! Oh no! I thought she was going to a temperance meeting this afternoon with the vicar but when she mentioned it, I never realised that it was going to take place in this hotel! Oh no! This is an absolute disaster.~~ I must get away from here. (PAUSE) ~~Just a sec - did my wife's message say which room her meeting was being held in?~~

ASTON : Yes. ~~She said quite distinctly it was in room Number Nine.~~ (PAUSE) ~~Oh, crikey! You realise what this means?~~

DAVIES : Yes. ~~It means that she's going to be on the landing looking for Number Nine at just the same moment that Fifi is also on the landing looking for Number Six! Oh crikey, what a mess!~~ (PAUSE) ~~Listen, there's only one thing for it. You must go and waylay Fifi in the lobby. Tell her some story, I don't care what, you'll think of something. Tell her I've been unavoidably delayed at the office, and then send her away.~~

ASTON : ~~That's easy enough to say, send her away. Where to? I mean, are you thinking of me taking her to another hotel where you can join her later? Is that your scheme? Because that assumes that you don't meet your wife when she arrives for her temperance meeting with the vicar.~~ (PAUSE) ~~I mean, it's five to three already and~~

DAVIES : ~~Then there's no time to spare. I've just remembered, the vicar is an absolute stickler for punctuality. I heard that from someone who was one of his parishioners when he worked in Sidcup. That means he's bound to be here early.~~ (PAUSE) ~~Oh no, and I've suddenly remembered something else! The man at the shop said he'd be delivering the inflatable woman to my room at the hotel round about three. And I've suddenly realised that I'm still wearing the kinky boots that I promised Fifi I would. Quick, quick!~~ Have you got any shoes?

ASTON : Shoes? (PAUSE) ~~Are you all right, old man?~~ Did you say shoes? (A KNOCKING IS HEARD AT THE DOOR OF THE ROOM. THERE IS A LONG SILENCE.) ~~Oh crikey, now we~~ really are in the soup. ~~Do~~

To The Milkman

God, when creating Man, at once decreed
That ample diet should supply our need
And proper eating, fed by proper food,
Should sickness from our mortal lives exclude.
He also, in His perfect plan, decrees
That thou shouldst carry forth thy milk & cheese
For thee to come unto my door with cream
Is but a part of His Eternal Scheme.
So, three pints, prithee, of thy lacteous flood,
Which willing udders yield to brace our blood,
And of that cheese, whose fame is widely known
Whose secret only Cheddar's sons do own.
(Made from the richness of emulsive fats
And churned e'en richer in their ligneous vats)
A half-pound, prithee, and of yellow cream
A half-pint, pray — but not that watery stream
Men know as "single" — no, the "double" sort
That can be whipped to pinnacles for sport,
As when the mighty waves, by Boreas lash'd,
Rise up in fury, till the rocks be splash'd,
And fearful mariners, that con the sky,
Do shake their head and wink their weather-eye,
All fearful to outface the furious storm,
While quick waves break, & then, as quick, reform
And trembling sailors can be heard to utter —
Oh, I forgot — add half a pound of butter.

PARTHENON·PAPYRUS·COMPANY·

DEAR·MR·PYTHAGORAS·

MANY·THANKS·FOR·
SUBMITTING·YOUR·DESIGN·WE·REGRET
TO·SAY·THAT·AS·AN·ENVELOPE, WE'RE·
AFRAID·IT'S·A·NON-STARTER—
YOURS·SINCERELY
S. MAMOPOULOS

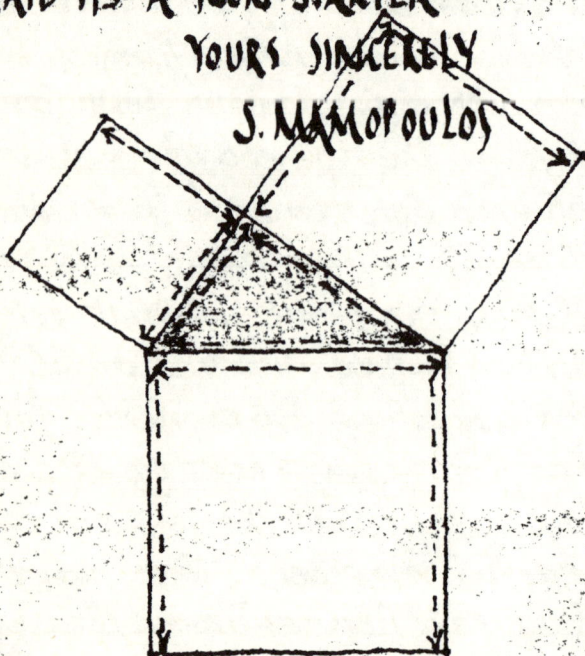

[Egyptologists differ about the precise
  meaning of this fragment, but the concensus
  seems to be that it is a shopping list and
  could be translated approximately as follows :
      " 1 chicken, 1 game of skittles for the
      kids, 1 hamburger, 2 more hambergers
      (or possibly balls for the game of skittles),
      2 fish, 2 meat cleavers, some eye drops(?),
      cheese and wine, 1 brassiere, 1 Cornish
      pasty (?), and don't forget the dogfood!"]

```
ESTHER (cont.) : but the Gas Board said :
1ST RESEARCHER : No comment.
ESTHER          : Sounds like the Gas Board is suffering from
                  an escape of hot air!
                  SIMPER WINSOMELY AT CAMERA.
                  RIDE LAUGHTER, THEN PUT ON SERIOUS FACE TO
                  MAKE THEM FEEL REALLY AWFUL FOR HAVING
                  LAUGHED.
                  But what about illness in children?
                  Do you know, even while you're watching this
                  programme, a lot of children are ill.
                  GIVE WRY EXPRESSION FOR A MOMENT WHILE THIS
                  SINKS IN.
                  Something to think about, isn't it?
                  LEAVE THEM FEELING AWFUL FOR A FEW MINUTES
                  LONGER, THEN BREAK THE MOOD BY CLASPING
                  KNEES AND SMILING WINSOMELY AGAIN.
                  But what about thinking? How much do people
                  think? In particular, how much do they
                  think at their most...intimate moments?
                  LEAVE A PAUSE FOR THE INNUENDO TO SINK IN.
                  Well, that's what we wondered, and that's
                  why we've been out and about on the streets
                  of London, asking people this simple question
                  What do you think about when you're on the
                  loo?
                  HOLD HAND TO MOUTH IN EXPRESSION OF DARING
                  AT THIS AMAZING BOLDNESS.
                  CUT TO FILM OF TOOTHLESS OLD LADY ROARING
                  WITH LAUGHTER AT MENTION OF THE WORD
                  "LAVATORY".
```

-17-

84

From CLARE RAYNER'S WASTEPAPER BASKET

Dear ....,

          Well, my oh my, you do seem to have got yourself into a state, don't you, love?

          You just take my word for it, you're not the only person in the world with that particular problem. Lots of people find themselves .... quite frequently, and very few of them suffer any ill effects. What you've got to do, love, is to stop worrying, talk to your partner about it, and if that doesn't help, then why don't you try ....?

          If you still find you're anxious after you've ...., then I suggest you get in touch with one of the specialist centres for this sort of trouble. Your nearest one is to be found at ....

          So cheer up, love. If things get really bad, you can always ring the Samaritans. Above all, love, remember – I really care about your problem, and you can always be sure of my continuing personal attention.

          Lots of love, love,

From RONALD REAGAN'S WASTEPAPER BASKET

I think you mean "UNCLEAR" here, Mr. President. Don't you?
J.T.S.

THE WHITE HOUSE, WASHINGTON D.C.
UNITED STATES OF AMERICA.

3rd March, 1986

Dear Mr. Gorbachov,
                    As we agreed last year in
Geneva, we live in a time when there are great
differences between our two nations, but I am
convinced that there must be a solution to
these differences. At the moment the precise
nature of this solution is (nuclear) but what
the hell, don't let's play for time - let's
get on with it. I'm sure between the two of us
we can put an end to the world's problems in
no time at all.
        I enclose a copy of Nancy's method of
preparing Hominy Grits, and she says she'd
sure be delighted to have Raisa's Borscht
recipe.
        Hoping to hear from you before you hear
from me,

                Yours sincerely,

                Ronald Reagan

PRESIDENT OF THE UNITED STATES OF AMERICA

WORDSEARCH

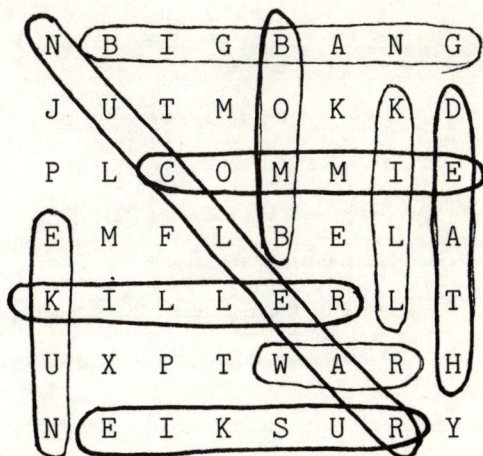

J. B. DEPALDO & SONS

Picture Cleaners & Restorers

17th August 1986.

Dear Mr. Richard,

    As requested, we have inspected the picture in your attic, but, since we cannot find any explanation for its rapid deterioration and the apparent aging of its subject, we regret that we are unable to take on the job of its restoration.

With apologies,

Yours sincerely,

DePaldo

GENERAL MANAGER

BUDGETTE
RENT-A-HORSE

Ye never know when
ye might neede a
goodly charger
and we do not
charge for over
twenty

our Superbe
four-houre
service. Aske for
detailes nowe—or
ye maye Live to
regrette it!

991 SEX

Screw , bang, bit, ride, grind, knock, mount, score, action, bunk-up, nookie, hump, bonk, jig-a-jig, how's your father, slap and tickle, legover, Ugandan discussions, knee-trembler, tupping, having it off, having it away, getting your end away, getting your rocks off, a bit on the side, a bit on a fork, a stab in the dark with a pork sword.

Wank   rub-up, jerk-off, play-off, massage, body rub, hand-job, J. Arthur, frig, flip-off, whack-off, wrist-job, pulling one's pudding, flogging one's mutton, tickling one's mutton dagger, pulling one's wire, pulling oneself off, pumping oneself off, playing with one's knob, shaking one's plum-tree, pulling the goose's neck, slinging one's jelly, flogging one's donkey, bashing one's bishop, trying to knock off the soldier's hat, it's all over my friend.

Vienna
11th March 1791.

My Dear Salieri

I've never written a fan letter before, but then I've never wanted to. However your music inspires me so much that I just have to write. If only I could write stuff as brilliant as yours

Many Congratulations

your devoted admirer

Wolfgang Amadeus Mozart

GALLIC PROVINCIAL COOKING

FROMAGE DE TETE

INGREDIENTS

    I HEAD
    I LB CARROTS
    I LB ONIONS
    I LB LEEKS
    III CLOVES GARLIC

METHOD

FIRST CLEAN THE HEAD
AND REMOVE ALL EXTRANEOUS
MATTER (HAIR, ETC) THEN
SOAK IN BRINE FOR THREE
DAYS IN A COOL PLACE BEFO
BOIL UP WITH THE VEGETAE
CHOPPED UP INTO SMALL PI
PINCH OF SALT AND CRUS
GARLIC UNTIL THE FLESH
SOFT TO THE TOUCH
REMOVE THE OUT
OFF THE BONE
UNTI

DEAR SCOTTIE
JUST NIPPING OUT
TO POINT FREDDIE AT
A FLOE! WON'T BE LONG
PLEASE MAKE SURE YOU
LEAVE THE TENT FLAP
OPEN, SO'S I CAN GET
BACK IN!
ALL THE BEST
OATESIE

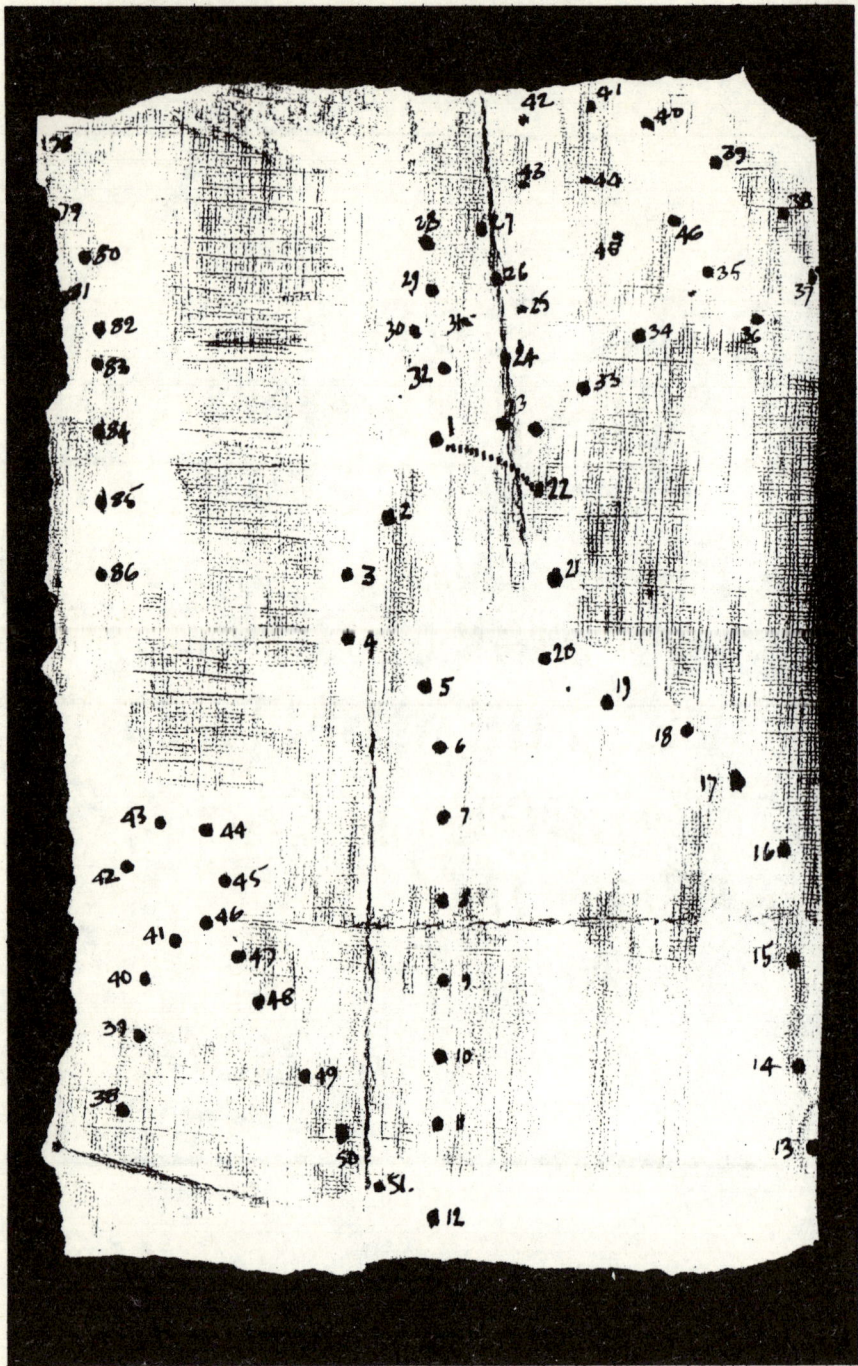

either you do something reall
nice for me {like write the odd
sonnet or something} or else
I'll tell 'm Hathaway what
you did to me last Tuesday
in ye Gents Publick Privie
Bradford - On - Avon I mean wh
I think about it.

Your Dark Laddie

XVIII

Shall I Compare Thee to a

Habitné
dapple bay
Hudson Bay
holiday
Saturday
Christmas day
popinjay
Lamp of Clay
Swiss chalet
cheese soufflé
Roundelay
Passion play
Consommé
Breakaway
Stowaway
Runaway
Castaway
Negligée
Old Bombay
Hiphooray

Your majesty, ~~it gives me enormous~~ you cannot imagine
~~how much~~ ~~pleasure~~ pleasure it gives me to
accept this ~~award~~ honour — not just because
it comes from you, but because it
represents the feelings of ~~my adoring~~ so many
~~public~~ other people.

You know, an ~~award~~ honour like this only
goes to one person, but, in a way
it's not just for one person. It is
applauding the work of so many others
— all those ~~highly skilled~~ very talented people who
don't often get in front of the
cameras, but whose contribution is
quite as — indeed, ~~frequently~~ sometimes —
far more ~~important~~ than my own.

And of those backroom geniuses,
I would like particularly to thank
my agent, without whose continual

From REV.W.A.SPOONER'S WASTEPAPER BASKET

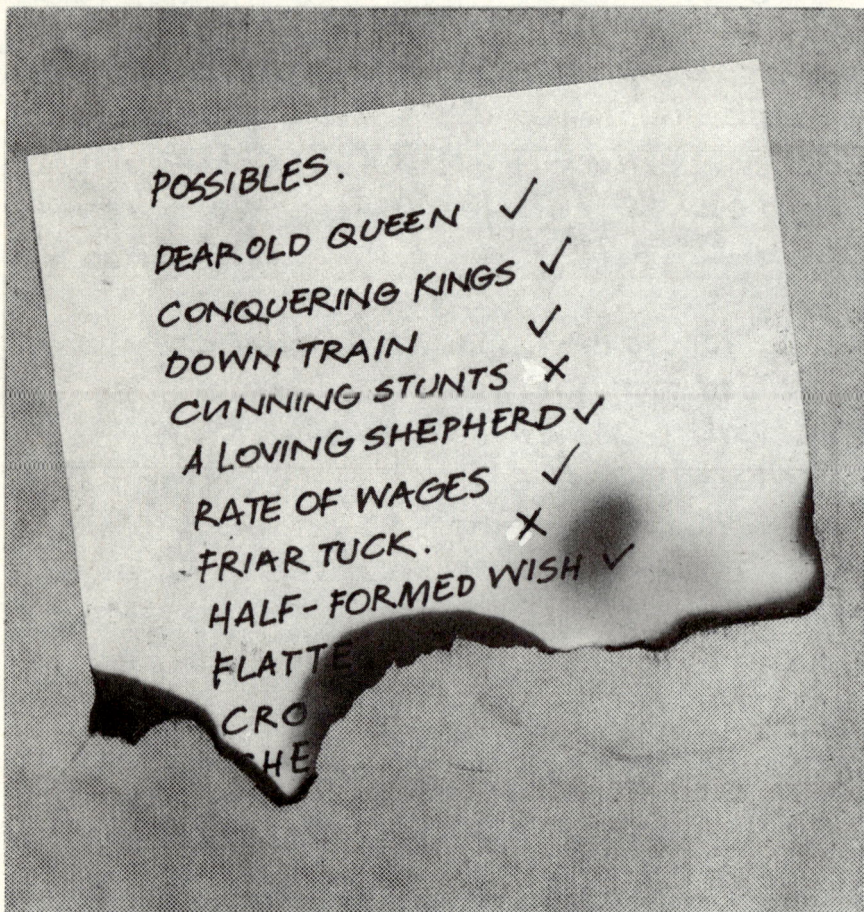

POSSIBLES.

DEAR OLD QUEEN ✓

CONQUERING KINGS ✓

DOWN TRAIN ✓

CUNNING STUNTS ✗

A LOVING SHEPHERD ✓

RATE OF WAGES ✓

FRIAR TUCK. ✗

HALF-FORMED WISH ✓

FLATT

CRO

HE

Praxton's Liver pills

3rd November 1869

Dear Mr Stanley

This is to confirm that our company will be happy to sponsor your forthcoming trip to Africa. We are well aware of the publicity value of your finding Dr Livingstone, and are happy to have our names associated with the enterprise.

We do not ask that you should carry any advertising material on your clothes and luggage. Our only request is that at the moment that you finally meet the object of your search you should greet him with the following words:

"Dr Livingstone, I presume you owe your survival in these terrible conditions to Praxton's Liver Pills?"

So long as these words are spoken (in full), we will be happy to pay all your expenses.

Yours Sincerely
J. Garrington
Marketing Manager.

Acme Firework Company

ST CATHERINE WHEEL LANE, LONDON E2.

2 April 1826

Dear Mr Stevenson

Thank you very much for showing us the plans for your proposed Rocket. We regret that we cannot possibly see how it is meant to fly, and are therefore unable to offer our backing to the project.

Yours Sincerely

J. Santos

On either side the river lie
Long fields of barley and of rye
That clothe the wold and meet
the sky;
And 'thro the field the road
runs by
To many-tower'd Camelot;
And up and down the people go,
Ta-tum-ta-tum-ta-tum-ti-toe
But I'm getting bored, and so
I'm sorry—that's Shalott!

Don't be facetious, Alfred
Bloody well <u>concentrate</u>!

⑦

and, you know,

LOOK SINCERELY AT CAMERA

I do understand what it feels like to suffer financial hardship.

DO THE OLD "ST. FRANCIS OF ASSISI" EXPRESSION

My parents weren't rich when I grew up.

LOOK FONDLY NOSTALGIC FOR LOST CHILDHOOD

No, times were hard. Times have always been hard for some of us.

EXPRESSION OF WRY ACCEPTANCE

But it's when times are hard that the people of this nation show the spirit that has made it a great nation!

DO THE OLD "FALKLANDS" FACE (CHIN RESOLUTELY UP, ETC.)

So when I hear people saying that this Government lacks compassion, that really hurts me.

LOOK SOULFUL (HINT OF A TEAR, MAYBE?)

Hurts me very deeply.

DO THE GREETING-SURVIVORS-OF-DISASTER FACE

LLANMAD   X

LLADOS   X

LLAKCUF   X

LLAREGGUB ✓

13, Larch Lane,
Leicester.
31st May
1982

Dear Ms. Townsend,

I hate to press
you but it is now six weeks
since I gave you my diary
for comment on its chances
of getting published, and
I would really quite like
it back now, as I want
to show it to John Tydeman
at the B.B.C. who has
expressed interest in my
writing after reading some poems

From LADY DIANA SPENSER

Friday

Dear Charles
        Thank you
very much for your letter.
Of course I was very
interested in your idea,
but I am afraid I am
    not that kind of girl.
    With me it has to
    be marriage or
    nothing!
        Love
        Diana
        xxx

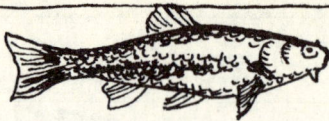

Venator : I thank you, good master. for this observation.
But I would know of you what shall be done when
your Angling is of no avail and you catch naught?

Piscator : Marry Sir, now must you learn, what many old
anglers know right well, that at some times, and
in some waters, be the rod never so supple, be he
that bears it never so subtle, and be the bait never
so succulent, no fish is to be got. And when
that be your fortune, must you take this course:
You must Lie.

Venator : Did you say "lie" good master?

Piscator : Sir I did say so: and by so doing, you will
follow the authority of Aristotle, of Pliny, of
Gesner, and of many others of credit.
And before I go farther in my discourse, let
me tell you, good scholar, of the divers
kinds or sorts of lies with which you must
arm yourself.

And, first, for the bigness of your catch.
Concerning which, I shall give you this direction:
that your fish shall thrive in bigness by much
discourse. It is said by Jovius, who hath
writ of fishes, that in an inn in Italy, he
did hear of a Carp of more than an
hundred pounds weight.

Venator : But, good master, did he see this prodigy with
his own eyes?

Piscator : Nay, good scholar, because you, that are but a
young angler, know not what Lying is. I will
now teach it to you. Let your lies be never
of the fish that is to be seen, but always of
the One That Got Away; and let this fish
be fully the length of your arms extended
sideways; for it has been observed by
Aldrovandus and divers other

LADY B: What — lost both your parents
Mr Worthing? Bad luck

What lost both your parents
Mr. Worthing? That's unfortunate.
It'd be bad enough if you'd only
lost one parent, Mr. Worthing.
Losing two's really tough.

To lose one parent, Mr. Worthing is
rotten luck. To lose two's even
worse.

To lose one parent, Mr Worthing, may
be considered rotten luck. To lose
both's even worse.

To lose one parent, Mr Worthing may
be regarded as rotten luck. To lose
both looks even worse

To lose one parent, Mr Worthing, may
be regarded as unfortunate. To lose
both looks like divine retribution.

To lose one parent, Mr Worthing, may
be regarded as a misfortune; to
lose both looks like the kind of
thing that only happens to someone
who's really accident-prone.

From VIRGINIA WOOLF'S WASTEPAPER BASKET

(Unfortunately, there is nothing available, since every last shopping list has already been published.)

I wandered lonely as
a cloud
That rains upon the
Daddies and the Mums
When all at once I saw
a crowd,
A host, of gold
chrysanthemums

I'm sorry William, I really
don't think you should go
on with this one, It's not
one of your best
Dorothy.

Dear Sir Christopher,
        Many Thanks
for your Design
I had my Dressmaker run it
up for me, but I fear it is
Mightily Uncomfortable. Nor
does it give me as much
Uplift as I Require

        Regretfully Yours

        Nell Gwynne

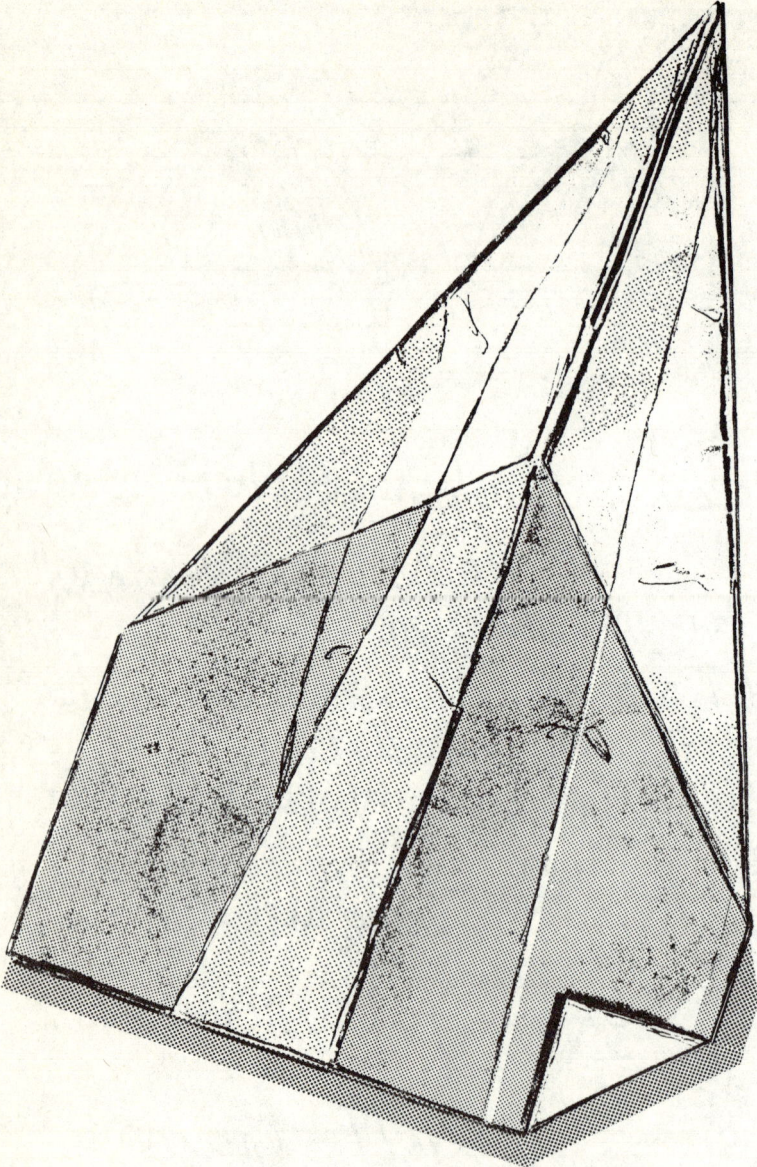